FUNERAL POEMS

Inspirational Death, Grief & Loss Poetry

Michael Ashby

thefuneralpoem.com
facebook-Death, Funeral, Bereavement Poems

First published in 2016
By thefuneralpoem.com
facebook.com/DeathFuneralBereavementPoems
Contact: via website.

CONTENTS

MODERN FUNERAL POEMS

FAMOUS FUNERAL POEMS 78

Public Comments from my website:

"You are truly gifted in what you do god bless you for allowing your self to be used as an instrument to minister to the broken hearted."

Daniel

"Thank you. I was looking at your beautiful website last night with tears in my eyes. Yes, I did notice the beautiful rainbows. They make me smile. Funny, but after a tragedy you begin to notice the smaller things in life, which then have meaning."

Louise Boyd

"Thank you for sharing my poem on this wonderful site. I enjoy reading the poems and finding peace. With all the trouble, sadness and uncertainty in the world it is wonderful to have a "go to" page to read the musings of like souls. God bless you for doing the work you do and for helping others have a place of release, a mental retreat to ease the pain of losing a loved one. Joy & God's blessings!"

Suzanne Simonovich

"Thank you for sharing your God-given gift with so many people. I will pray for your continued strength."

Rose Duffy

"I have read through a couple of poems the cup of tea and the mobile phone and found them uplifting... i only started trying to write 2 years ago after a loss which affected me greatly and this is a breath of fresh air...tyvm" **Karen**

THE BEACH OF HUMAN ANGUISH

Every second of every day
A tsunami of mortal loss
Crashes blindly onto
The beach of human anguish
Driven by howls of unimaginable pain

To be eventually calmed by
The huge cornerstones of family
Loved ones, friends... and
For some, religious beliefs

My poems are the smallest
Grain of sand on that beach
But even they glisten from

A teardrop now and again

Michael Ashby

A BRIEF MATTER

Life is
Short
But death
Takes
A heartbeat

Michael Ashby

A CRICKETER'S LAST BOUNDARY

Weeping willows formed an honour guard
For the cricket ball writ with a noble name
A team of ten, which had once been eleven
Would never be the same side again

No bails united the forlorn stumps
Since this wicket had fallen some days ago
And as the bowler delivered to the lone batsman
The hushed crowd willed for a six to go

The magical sound... of leather on willow
The sweet smell... of freshly cut grass
A cricketer... crossing the last boundary
To a third innings that would forever last

Michael Ashby

At the Thanksgiving Service in memory of Damian D'Oliveira, Worcestershire County Cricket Club's "current President and former player John Elliott read the moving Michael Ashby poem A Cricketer's Last Boundary". "Damian, a Worcestershire player for 13 years from 1982-1995 and then Academy Director from 2000 onwards, passed away... after a long and brave battle against cancer."

From: wccc.co.uk

A GODDESS AWAITS

Her current recharges India
Her waters cleanse souls
All hail Mother Ganga
Welcome home, welcome home

Michael Ashby

A LEAP OF FAITH

I was coming home
I was coming home to die
I was coming home to die
In my own bed

Although buoyed by this hope
I could feel my strength ebbing
As I struggled against the tide of life
That had finally turned against me

Suddenly, the world erupted
Into turbulence and confusion
I had reached the last hurdle
I would now have to overcome

With all the power remaining
In my mortal being
I leapt free from earth's pull
And soared through the air

I am McSalmon
Of the Salmonidae

I was home
I was home to die
I was home to die
In my own bed

Michael Ashby

Public Comments from my facebook page:

Tirthankar Raychaudhuri *magnificient.*

Jessica Arora *oh so sad, but soo beautiful...*

Dileep Naik *So nice n touchy*

Anjan Chakraborty *Nice concoction & resemblance made with the inevitable death*

Debangshi Satapathy *Very touching*

A LONG CUP OF TEA

Death is too negative for me
So I'll be popping off
For a long cup of tea
Do splash out
On two bags in the pot
And for my god's sake
Keep the water hot
Please pick the biggest mug
You can find
Because size really does matter
At this time
I'll pass on the Lapsang
With that Souchong
And that stuff with bergamot
And stick with my favourite friend
You know the English breakfast blend
Breakfast! thanks for reminding me
There's just time before I fail
To stand on ceremony
(Two rashers of best smoked back
Should keep me smelling sweet
Up the smoke stack)
So, mother, put the kettle on for me
It's time, mother, for my long cup of tea

Michael Ashby

Public Comments from my website:

We've written a play about two sisters: one has just died though appears as one of the two characters in the play. She has left a letter of instructions for her sister about funeral arrangements, including asking her to read a poem. The sister considers various options then chooses your 'A long cup of tea'.

Susan (Leather) and Lesley (Sherwood)

PS We're taking the play to the Edinburgh Festival Fringe this August 2013

*(**Sadly**, December 2015, Sue passed away. Lesley read "A Long Cup Of Tea" to over 200 family and friends at a ceremony on January 9th to remember her wonderful life... 'An extraordinary person, who left us far too soon').*

"I found your poem 'A long cup of Tea' on your website and thought it might do rather well as part of my eulogy for my best Friend who passed away at the end of November 2012.

As it was to be read out in church, I changed a few words and amended the last half to make it personal to him

That has now passed and the poem went down rather well.

My friend would go around to his mothers' flat every weekday, when he wasn't working and sit with her watching afternoon quiz shows on TV with a nice cup of tea. I especially wanted to explain this as some of his friends thought he was a bit of a drinker, actually he liked his tea."

Richard Peabody

"My mother died recently. She was ALWAYS making cups of tea, M&S Gold Blend English Breakfast, which she never finished. At her funeral, your lovely, very apt poem was read out by our son. It brought much comfort to those of us listening who knew her. Thank you.

Sue H.

Hello, can I use your poem "A Long Cup of Tea" for my Death Cafe on 2nd November...not sure how I'll use it, may even put it on my flyer.

Paula Rainey Crofts

(You are very welcome to use my poem.)

Public Comments from my facebook page:

Karen Bradley Colweck *Perfect for my British Mum who will always miss her Son, Kevin. Until we all meet again, on the other side.xoxoxo*

Alison Hellinikakis *Lovely poem. Big hugs too you.xxx*

Jane Sansom *Let's hope Muriel and Walter have now had their long overdue cuppa together!*

Christine McGhee *It`s almost a perfect tribute for my dad. Is it ok to use and to adapt it slightly?*

(You are most welcome)

Sharon Sosa *Pretty*

Alice M Flowers *Beautiful.*

ANGELS

Feathers flying from God's heavenly nest
White winged wonders, on their Earthly quest
God's too busy to help you today
So your angels are on their way
Just look out, for the signs are there
The kiss of a breeze in the still night air
A magical cake lighting up children's eyes
A double rainbow in cloudless skies
All bridging the gap between heaven and you
As we toast absent friend, while memories renew

Michael Ashby

A MISCARRIAGE OF JUSTICE

Death is guilty
Life is innocent
But death delivers
A life sentence

Michael Ashby

- FEELINGS/EMOTIONS
  - unfairness of death
  - p. 10
  - p. 9.

BINGO

My mum's playing Bingo in heaven
With a happy smile on her face
If she'd known there was a Bingo hall in
heaven
She'd have looked more forward to the place

Past 78 and heaven's gate
It's 83 and time for tea
With 61 and a baker's bun
And no queue for the lavatory

After 41 and time for fun
She's won with 54 and wiped the floor
I really do thank my lucky stars
My mum landed in heaven instead of on mars

Michael Ashby

CALMER

Death, pain, hopelessness
Zen
M e d i t a t e
B r e a t h e
K a r m a
E n l i g h t e n m e n t
P e a c e

Michael Ashby

CHRIST THE REDEEMER

The grieving pilgrim
Prayed in the darkness. Jesus
Shone out with his love

Michael Ashby

CONDOR

To reach heaven on
A wing and a prayer, gods
Created condor

Michael Ashby

CRUISING THE SUPERNOVA

The sailor cast off the mortal coil
As the voyage of a lifetime was hatched
And the astral yacht blew off the Beaufort scale
At a speed no lifeboat could match

With star boards current in every direction
And solar winds blowing sternly on the face
The sailor waved and bowed to mother earth
Before joining a round the universe race

Michael Ashby

Speerfte

DO NOT BE AFRAID

The Liffey drowned in Irish tears
Guinness heads rose sober and bowed
The Blarney stone kissed our noble poet farewell
As the soil of Bellaghy stood welcoming and
proud

Michael Ashby

(In remembrance of Seamus Heaney, Poet)

FORTIFYING THE SPIRITS

When the bell rings for last orders
Please don't panic or get vexed
It's simply time to sup this world's last drink
Before ordering your first in the next

It's always opening time in heaven
And the alcohol doesn't go to your head
It floats around in one's ether
And fortifies your spirit instead

The dinosaur scratchings are slightly chewy
And the Martian wine's an unfriendly red
But not peeing in the night is pure delight
And leaves you longer to hang over your bed

Your angel's share is there to be asked for
Of the malt whisky escaped from oak casks
You can savour a peaty Macallan '46
For a drink that will forever last

"The Traveler's Rest" always welcomes
departed drinkers
With a warm smile and a kindly nod
You'll never have to put your hand in your pocket
again
Because this really is a free house, thank god

Michael Ashby

- lots of poems specific to professions & passions -
- lovely one-liners

FUNERALISSIMO

The musical notes stood in lines
Discordant in their grief
Before regaining their composure
As black tears in embossed relief

The instruments played this salutation
To a musician of note and much more
At the end, everyone stamped their feet
Encore, Encore, Encore

Michael Ashby

Public Comments from my facebook page:

April O'sullivan *In memory of my mother who died 14 years ago today x*

Tinongannabelle Navarro *in loving memory of my dad who died 19 of feb.2013*

GALAPAGOS

I'm back as a Galapagos tortoise
To dwell
Having fired my wrinkly
Human shell

I'm recycling my naturally
Adventurous spirit
With yet another Earthly
Planetary visit

Michael Ashby

GAME, SET AND MATCH

I always dreamt of winning Wimbledon
And lifting the trophy on centre court
But the highest umpire has called me out
Sorry, but it's game, set and match, old sport

I'd love - 15 minutes more... to ace strawberries and cream
I'd love - 30 minutes more... to be served more champagne than I aught
I'd love - 40 minutes more... to rally with you all
Sorry, but it's game, set and match, old sport

Michael Ashby

GHOSTS OF THE FALLEN

The ghosts of the fallen are all agreed
Something may be wrong with the warrior's creed
For a shot of death brings icy clarity
And deep, deep sadness to a new reality
Where there's no way forward and there's no way back
To life before the last bloody attack
Knowing families and friends lie waiting in their homes
To be shot through their heads with their telephones

At peace at last in the universe
About just one question the ghosts converse
To put to the ones whose orders were writ
Was the loss of our lives really worth it?

Michael Ashby

GLASTONBURY

You're all on God's conveyor belt
You're heading for a fall
But heaven's got no gravity
So I'm dancing above you all

Work out what you want from life
And make your dreams come true
You could
Watch the sun rise on pyramids
Or set on Uluru
You could
Walk on China's greatest wall
Or trek to Timbuktu
You could
Aim high upon the Eiffel tower
Or higher at Machu Picchu

You're all on God's conveyor belt
You're heading for a fall
But heaven's got no gravity
So I'm dancing above you all
Your music's singing in my soul
As I sway on the Tor above
But beyond all that I've said before
I just hope that you find love

Michael Ashby

GOD BLESS YOU BEAUTIFUL CHILDREN

God bless you beautiful children
God bless you every one
Humanity will never forget you
Each daughter and each son
Our days and nights are darker now
That your light has moved on
God bless you beautiful children
We listen for your heavenly song

Michael Ashby

GOLDEN MOMENTS

My life has been a mirage
Built on shifting sands
And now my time of liquid gold
Has flowed from my hands

The precious seconds, minutes and hours
The priceless weeks, months and years
End in my new oasis
With welcoming forbears

Michael Ashby

Public Comment from my facebook page:

Alice M Flowers *Beautiful.....heart felt!*

GOOD GOD

Do I
Believe in God
Does God
Believe in me

Although I am
Unsure about God
I am sure
A good God
Would be sure
About me

Michael Ashby

GRANDPA'S LOST HIS GR

My grandpa has lost his gr
And gone to 'andpa land
It's where all the tired 'andpas go
When they depart the family band
So now whenever I'm hurt
Or my troubles are too much for me
I remember sitting up on my grandpa's knee
Safe within his grandpa zone
All in a little world of our own
With wisdom, patience, humour and guile
There's nothing that couldn't be sorted
by grandpa's smile
Boys will be boys
And men will be men
But only the best of them
End up as grandpas in the end
If you ever hear the roar of thunder, late at night
Don't hide under your duvet, out of sight
Someone's just left open
The 'andpa land door
And boy, Oh boy
A herd of 'andpas
Can't half snore

Michael Ashby

Public Comment from my facebook page:

Olay Columbretis *I had also a grandpa who loved my twin and me so much. Now I will be 60 but not a single day in my life that I had not think of my dearest grandpa.*

HEAVEN ON EARTH

I was passing through Utopia
On my way to Nirvana
When I saw a sign
Pointing back to Heaven

Where I'd been, all along

Michael Ashby

HOOK, LINE AND SINKER

As I sat upon a rock
With the waters breaking around me
I pondered matters of life and death
A-fishing by the sea
I was waiting for the tide to come in
Which would drown others in despair
So let me reassure you now
How much I've enjoyed being a being here

I know you know I'm still spinning lines
To help you on land at this time
Please swallow them hook, line and sinker
Because you're the real catch of me the fisher

Michael Ashby

I AM NOT GONE

I am not gone, while you cry with me
I am not gone, while you smile with me
I am not gone, while you remember with me
I will come, when you call my name
I will come, when I feel your pain
I will come, on your final day
It could never be, that we, would never be
We shall always, be together, forever
I AM NOT GONE
Michael Ashby
Public Comments from my facebook page:
John Felix *Michael, thank you for this lovely post...! It's beautiful, will help many to handle death with courage...*
Charito Laitan Marquez *O how inspiring these messages of poems you shared.thank you,thank you for awakening my soul.*
Ravish Kumar *Thank you so much Sir for this lovely post.....*
Feeling good inside after reading this... Thank you
Lyn Angel Ompoc *..SO NICE..TOUCHES MY HEART..THANKS TO THE EDITOR..FOR SHARING,.GOD IS GOOD ALL THE TIME,,,*
Athenna Bernadine Corpuz *I like your poem its like pain reliever to someone who lost a son .*
Dhana Brooks-Christian *What beautiful and comforting words.For my son Chase Christian. I love you baby boy.*

Victoria Sula Toledo *When i read this . I remember my son.. i cry and cry . Son wheever u r we miss u so much... love u*
Fatima Palafox *Lost my dear son,2 yrs.hence,in cag.de oro.limketkai, bomb blast!!!....thank you for sharing a beautiful poem..."medical convention event"i sincerely feel greatly for d families n wives, who lost their loveones, tragically.1 pray that, they will find comfort in Gods'Love , n Streght in d Holy Spirit, n Trust wd Hope in His Loving Kindness...*
Sundara Vadivel *after reading this poem iam thinking of my son tejas from malaysia. when i will meet him? i decided my final destination. before taking that decision just want to meet my son.*
Julie-ann dela Roca *I still believe that my mom is not really gone even though she died infront of me..thanks for this poem..*
Steffini L. Haus *Love this, in memory of my mom Marilyn I. House who passed on 11/29/14 and was put into mother earth on 12/2/14 Tuesday. Thank you for sharing ...*
Nerissa Rico Sicat *This is true! I like this poem.when my mama was lost i lost everything! But still i have to accept the fact that no one is exemted in Death.*
Jènéfër Jèny *I feel so much pain when my mother pass away .. and after reading this peom I believe that my mother is not really gone ...*
Shikha Singh *V nice my mother use to speak*

like this to me she was most lovable to me
France Leafcarl del Castillo *I read all the poem, I fell my tears go down.I miss my father so much, and I believe he always with me.,.I ask him to guided all my sister and brother to the right paths.if they did a wrong path, they can saw my father in thier dream, yes it's really happened.thank you lord Jesus to hold my father...I always pray his soul to be peace and to be with you...thank you this post.*
Bheng Tating *reading this poem made me teary eyed...miz my daddy vry much ;(tnx for this post, God Bless*
Luzviminda Galon Rato-sahi *We lost our beloved PapA and Manoi Jose and we that they are not gone but they are ahead of us. That someday we will meet in heaven.Thank you for this poem.*
Margarita Soriano Samonte *So true, so touching when i started reading it my tears began to fall, I remember my husband who passed away recently. And it pained me. I love and miss him so much. My only consolation is knowing that he feels no pain now and he's w/ our Lord. Thanks for sharing your poem.*
Chandrani Banerjee Bhattacharya *It's a beautiful poem..reminding me all the beautiful moments I shared with my beloved husband.... I miss him a lot*
Manalo Christina *Its true!!i feel my beloved husband.Love i misss u sooooooo much!i love you*

so..........
Madhava Gopal *I lost my wife 3 months back.I think these lines were written for me. Thank you .*
Felipe Joaquin Sr. *This qoute is for my beloved wife who had just passed away.My love i do miss u a lot wherever u are you remain forever in our hearts.We love you.May you rest peacefully thru the hands of our Lord,amen.*
Albarica Benitez *I lost my big brother 24 years ago but the pain remain inside my heart.. I know the word 'move on'...but i don't know how to do it.. I know that my brother is in heaven right now.. thank u for ur post.. Its really wonderful.*
Noel Agregado Bejo *A message for enlightenment to our dear brod molong armada who has just lost his beloved mother.condolence bro.*
Doris V Cordero *i love this poem made me tear up in honor and memory of my brother who commited sucide oct 4 marked his anniversary death. and this poem is perfect*
Jacob Imperial Lozada *In remembrance of my departed sister Phoebe Alyssa Tianga Imperial, we love you forever.*
Marife Gutierrez *I will not be gone for I stayed in your heart. You remember me because you wanted to be part of my life. If not, why bother remember my face for in your eyes it was miracles. Never would I be lost if you find the*

true me..
Felipe Joaquin Sr. *Very touching verse,i remember my love who passed away 9 mos.ago.nice sharing your post.*
Geraldine Samperoy *Gosh,i super love poem..wow.*
Reyna Dubhe Famularcano Rodolfo *This poem I remember our Lord our Savior.I was blessed.*
Isabella Totoh *I rmmbr da tm of laughters,tears n pains bt hearing diz evn dou m still sad it maks me relift I MIZZZI U!!*
Jyoti Bhardwaz *i read all the poem..i fell my tears go down.i miss my all friends*
Nerie Saldivar *It touches my heart i feel it!! smile emoticon*
Rosemarie Martinez *I mean, if I told this to my family, they won't hide under their blankets. Just a thought...*
Raquel de Leon *When i die i dont want to see them cry .,,im not gone.....always and forever that in every step they make i am there for them......love you my children and apos*
Hermie Gabilan Galorio *My father died oct 21 2015 he slways live in my heart forever i love u papa . and i love this poem touch my heart and soul ,i know that my GOD bring him to heaven*
Shallani Anschuetz Singh Thakur *I wonder why people cry when someone died, u should not cry but rather than be thankful because he/she rest in other dimension*

IN THE LINE OF DUTY

In the fight between good and evil
Sometimes a sacrifice is made

In the line of duty
Sometimes a life is laid
Down
Forever
In the hearts of the thinner blue line

To protect and serve the public
The life, just given, was mine

Michael Ashby

(When posted on Facebook, this poem was Liked by the Scottish Police Memorial Trust and the National Police Memorial - Australia.)

I WANT TO BE BURIED WITH MY MOBILE PHONE

I want to be buried with my mobile phone
So I can ring in the changes at my new home
With central heating and a marble en-suite
And lots of thermal socks for my poor cold feet
I'll be able to give in to a takeaway
And watch favourite movies on a rainy day
And if I'm feeling a bit under the weather
I'll talk to you until I begin to feel better
I've got party hats, fairy cakes and songs to sing
In case somebody should chance to drop in
Which is much more likely than you'd think
As my coffin roof is on the blink

I'll be leaving you now as I've got a waiting call
It's from my new friend over by the cemetery wall
I watched the service yesterday through my periscope
They buried him with his mobile, their little joke
But he'll have the last laugh, when his bill drops through their door
Fourteen hundred and forty minutes a day, for eternity and evermore **Michael Ashby**

Public Comments from my facebook page:

Beverly McGovern Bailey *I buried my husband with his cell phone, he was always talking to someone. Wish I could talk with him.*
Josie Mackness *this is lovely lite hearted xxx*
Cath Lynas Lever *Love it. In this day it is very appropriate*

JUST IN CASE

I wonder if
My atheist friend
Risked a quick prayer
Right at the end

Just in case
He was wrong
After all
About what would happen
After his last
Curtain call

Finally realizing
That I might
Just be right
And that he
Wasn't alone
On his longest night

Michael Ashby

LIFE AND DEATH AND LIFE

Dying leaf kisses
Bark of crying tree, farewell
Sweet blossom for now

Michael Ashby

(Adapted for the Qingming Festival.)

REPAYING OUR ROOTS

Dying leaf kisses
Branch of crying tree, farewell
Sweet blossom for now

Michael Ashby

LIFE GOES ON

I want fireworks at my funeral
To brighten up your eyes
I want clowns at my funeral
To return all your smiles

I want dancing at my funeral
To help you move along
I want a party at my funeral
Filled with your happy throng

So, party, party, party
And cheer my spirit with song
As my last wish is you celebrate
That life goes on

Michael Ashby

LIFE SCULPTURE

When god poured me
From his perfect mould
He forgot to tell me
That I would grow old
My skin would wrinkle
My hair would turn grey
And that even my sweet tooth
Would decay

Dear god please
Take pity on me
And recast me in
Your foundry
A magnificent bronze
As smooth as can be
No lines. no grey
Just perfect immortality

Michael Ashby

MADIBA (Nelson Mandela) AND THE LION

The lion sprang up the staircase on fire
As the African night began to die
A neon hospital sign flickered a warning
Before failing against a bloody dawn sky

The champion warrior shed his gown
And held firm the proffered mane in his hands
With a roar that would shake the entire world
They leapt as one for heavenly lands

Michael Ashby
Public Comments from my facebook page:
Mpfuni Rock-Nation *R.I.P Lion of Africa...*
Lebogang Shakezito Nshingila *Our hero O Tata Madiba Lion of da nation*
Tolakele Stanction Tk Matebese *Aahh Dalibhunga*
Kesebelwang Jas *Lala ngoxolo Tata u wil alwyz be rmbd n we wil alwz luv u 4evr.*
Sylvia Letaoana *Rest in peace tata u ll always be remembered.*
Shepard Mhlanga Shepi *rest in peace you done good job thank you madiba.*
Rozelene Violet Wolff *RIP Madiba we pray ur Dreams for South Africa will continue that we can all live as one in this beautiful land of ours*

MAYA ANGELOU

True poets never die
Their body of work
Breathes through
Their touching words
Forever

Michael Ashby

Public Comments from my facebook page:

Sushmita Mukherjee *Brilliant Maya! The radiance of the essence, shines through her words...forever.... Thanks for sharing...expressing through beautiful words, the tribute.... Warm regards,*

Linda Hopkins *Maya touched a lot of soul's. Her Legacy will live on through her poetry*

Tammie Turner *Gorgeous just like her may she rest in peace ill miss her deeply*

Connie Cornetto Mofokeng *may she RIP*

Evelyn Robles *She will be sorely missed by the world.*

Jeanine Johnson *Deep*

MILKING THE MOMENTS

We only have today
In fact, we only have now
It's such a chilling thought
I'm so glad I'm not a cow

My insides would churn
And turn into ice cream
I would be the biggest milkshake
That the world had ever seen

We only have today
In fact, we only have now
I'm so glad I milked my moments
But I'm even gladder I wasn't a cow

Michael Ashby

MY ECO DEATH

I was lying naked.... in a woodland glade
(The hedgehog ball heard its last foxtrot)
Covered by branches.... of modest shade
(The nightingale blew out her candle)
On a bed of.... the softest moss
(The owl closed a squeaking dormouse)
Beneath a leafy blanket.... sharing my loss
(The queen bee was stung, by the sweet kiss of death)
Time to reflect.... after time to dwell
Surrounded by nature's.... dingly dell

My monitor's alarm.... the air did shell
And nurses rushed in.... to cancel the bell
An angelic smile.... a machine's last pips
A sigh of contentment.... escaping my lips

Peace.... Oh blessed peace
Peace.... at last

Michael Ashby

MY LAST ASSEMBLY

If this life has taught me anything
It's that I've been a student all my days
Learning from each interaction
Along the scholastic way

Now a place in the open universe awaits, and
The answer to the last question of the exam hall
Are my views on Religious Education
Still worth anything at all

So farewell to you and my verbosity
I now end with one of Charles Eliot's jots
'A good teacher is like eternity
He/She never knows where his/her influence stops'

Michael Ashby

MY LIGHT WILL SHINE FOREVER

Synapses, lightening forks
Neural nets cast aglow
My being is no longer earthed
As across space I flow

Eternally charged with immortal life
I feel the pull of people past
My light will shine forever
And for you will everlast

Michael Ashby

MY MUM

Where did it go?
My mother once asked
As the clock tick-tocked
And her life flew past
In the race against time
She led for most of the way
But the track was endless
Unlike her last day
(Take care of your father
Promise you will
As she passed on the baton
She would never spill)
So polish the stars
And fire up the sun
And put out some slippers
To welcome my mum
Find a new galaxy
And light up her name
Because life on planet Earth
Just won't be the same

Michael Ashby
Public Comments from my facebook page:
Kelly Tyree Hale *I totally relate to this since losing my mom when I was 15 to cancer. Almost 40 now. Pain is just as real as it was then. Thank you for sharing this. Its beautiful*
Tracy Mclean *ill dedicate this wan to ma wee mammy who a still miss even though its been ten*

yrs a think about her everyday or a say things she used to say miss her smile and i try and look after my wee Dad as well xxXxxx cheers Marie nice one X

Pamela R. Curtis *Wow*

Megan Hughes*That is beautiful thank you made me cry a bit xxx*

Reba Stafford *Beautiful!*

Reba Stafford *Miss you mama, miss you Arlene*

Jacqueline Kane *That is just beautiful thanks for sharing*

Elizabeth Snowden *Thank you that is beautiful.*

Demetra Sturdivant *Touching and beautiful*

Margaret Mills *This is lovely Jake had a wee greet for both our mums lolx rabble xx*

Gordon Young *That's lovely*

Margaret Keast *Tasha that is so lovely x*
Hayley Kingwell *Beautiful but now I'm blabbing on the bus, thinking of you x*

NASHVILLE ON GOD'S RADIO

Put spurs on the foot of my coffin
Put my comfiest boots on my feet
Put my hat on to face the future down
Then ride out to my final meet

We'll take a last ride together
We'll get dust and tears in our eyes
We'll sleep out in the moonlight
And count our blessings under the skies

We'll share a last swig of whisky
We'll share the last beans from the pot
We'll sing round dying embers
Until my last ride has to stop

Then I'm off to ride god's rodeo
Where I'll tame my new bronc-eo
With Nashville on god's radio
I'll be riding shooting stars

Michael Ashby

OFF TO THE RACES

I'm off to the races in heaven
In fact, I'm champing at the bit
At the prospect of wagering that Arkle
Will give Desert Orchid the slip

Satellite TV's a safe bet to view
The next Cheltenham Gold Cup
From my new, free 'Hi-Lux Chalet'
I'll be wishing you the best of luck

I've given life a good run for my money
But it's time to say 'Cheerio' for now... old sports
I'm looking forward to catching up with you all again... one day
Over a glass of your favourite champagne or port

Michael Ashby

Poem in response to
Public Comment from my website:
"Do you have any suitable poems / prayers / short comments for the funeral of a keen racegoer who has just died aged 85? His regular courses were Wincanton and Cheltenham and TV. Many thanks." ***James Joicey-Cecil***

OLD AGE ISN'T FOR WIMPS

It's a lonely fight
In the middle of the night
With the temperature falling
And old pains calling

Pains in the body
Pains in the soul
Old age sometimes
Can be a living hell

Michael Ashby

ONE LAST FLUTTER

I've always gone with the roll of the dice
But now my numbers up
And since I'm the one down below
There must be six up top

I always knew the odds were against me
So it's time for one last flutter and sin
I'm going to bet on heaven not hell
God knows if I'll end with a win

Michael Ashby

PUT OUT TO SEED AGAIN

It's my turn now to be planted
Put out to seed again
While the fruits of my earthly labours
Flourish in the sun and rain

It's a wonderful day to be planted
In rich, deep loamy soil
A natural bed, for a tired gardener's head
With green fingered hands of toil

Please plant a tree or bush for me
To celebrate a gardener's life ways
I strove to enrich the world with beauty
Over many, many gardening days

Michael Ashby

RAINBOWS ON THE MOON

There are rainbows on the moon
There are clouds in outer space
The night has started mourning
Since I passed away too soon

There are rainbows on the moon
There are colours crying in tiers
The solar wind is wailing
Since I passed away too soon

I shine with the Northern Lights
I shine with the waning moon
I shine with the shooting stars
Since I passed away too soon

Now one zillion candles
Are shining all around me
One zillion and one candles
For my life on earth to see

Michael Ashby

Public Comments from my facebook page:
Erlina Gonzales Sta Maria *How i miss my only son ...shine on us my beloved son*

Ginger Calvert *I talk to you Ethan in the night to the stars because I know you are one*

Marilou Loilo *to my niece and nephew who passed away too soon., they are now the auroras*

Cora Leveriza *Reminds me of john paul hendrix my grandson who passed away so soon at age 19. Gone but never forgotten*

Julieta Magsilang-Lopez *Ohh i missed somuch my hubby who passed away so soon*

Aivie Palenzuela *Thats light never died anymore ,coz that light guide and change the darkness in our life to see what i and u could be*

Rebecca Williams *To my brother and my beloved Jeff, passed away too soon ....never forgotten*

Julieta Magsilang-Lopez *Ohh i missed somuch my hubby who passed away so soon*

REMEMBRANCE SUNDAY

I left my legs on the battlefield
But I will still stand tall
I left my arms on the battlefield
But I will still salute you all
I left my nerve on the battlefield
But I will not tremble or fall
From the first firing of the field gun
To the dying breath of the "Last Post" call

Michael Ashby
Public Comments from my facebook page:
June Bowley *Beautiful words will never forget Amen*
Mary McCann *My grandad came home left his leg in battle always stood with him to remember*
Monica Sankey *Amen ,to my Granddad and all brave Soldiers ,and what a nice poem .AMEN*
Gill Jones *We will remember them.very moving poem and picture.thank you for sharing it with us.x*
Rachel Grist *Amen a very true and moving poem # leastweforget #neverforget Thankyou to all who risk their lives to protect us from the troubles of past and present who never backed down who proudly fought for this country more should be done to help each and everyone of those coming back from war and their families it isn't a easy time and it is the least we can do xxxxxxx*

SALCOMBE'S ESTUARY ORCHESTRA

Seabirds dance to Neptune's beat, and
Like moths around a flame
Welcome back the fishing fleet
Back safe from the catching game

In and out, to and fro
Rise and fall, high and low
Flood tide, ebb tide, spring tide and neap tide
Riverside, seaside, creek side and boat side
All dance to the waters' refrain
And while cormorants line up to conduct
The estuary orchestra plays again

Ferries crossing, visitors jostling
Lights blinking, prawns winking
Sails bracing, dinghies racing
Bobcats leaping, seadogs sleeping
Boatmen waving, lifeboat saving

Finally, the conductors dry
Immodestly on a prow
And, as the sun turns off the rain
The estuary orchestra takes a bow
Before playing a tidal encore
Over and over and over again

Michael Ashby

SLEEPING 'AU NATUREL'

When there are more days behind you
Than those that lie ahead
Now really isn't the time
To be a-lying long in one's bed
So, kick off the covers
Go on, you I dare
Throw open the windows
And drink in deep of the fresh air
But if you sleep 'au naturel'
Please do take a care
Lest your neighbour has a weak heart
And a proclivity to stare

Michael Ashby

SUN ARISE

God woke his sun
For me this morning
Just for me
Just for me
And set about
The sea awarming
Just to see
Just to see
How he, me
His sun and the sea
Could just be
Could just be
How he, me
His sun and the sea
Could just be

Michael Ashby

Public Comment from my website:
"I like this poem. I was on line searching for an American Indian poem regarding death for my friend Bob to read at his mom's funeral who loved the American Indians. As I write this she's still alive, but will be gone in a few days."
Betsy Pellitteri

SWAN SONG

The swan silently
Crossed the river
No reflection, no ripple
In her wake
Lit by a moving sunbeam
She crossed the water
Just, for my sake

I sat down aboard her back
As her head turned to me
And she looked deeply into my eyes, asking
Are you really, really, ready
I nodded, as tears rained, from my face
To join countless others in their river

The swan started swimming
And slowly singing
The most beautiful music
I had ever heard in my life
And then the swan
Suddenly changed, from black
Into a dazzling white
And I stopped crying, and started smiling
As together, we crossed over
Into the most brilliant of light

Michael Ashby

TEARS IN MY HEART

All the tears in my heart
Will only dry when I die
When new tears of happiness
Are reborn in all our eyes

Michael Ashby

Public Comments from my facebook page:

Olay Columbretis *this poem tells that there is so much to hope for, in spite of our tears. a poem so comforting*

Rhea Mae Lapirap Dayot *Tears in my heart will be there forever.,.,i love you so much*

THE CLUTHA VAULTS

It could have been me
It could have been you
That perished in Glasgow
Under a bolt from the blue

The randomness of this tragedy
Near takes one's breath away
And unites us all in grieving
On this memorial day

We salute selfless fighters
Who battled to save from the fray
And will always remember the fallen
Who in The Clutha Vaults together lay

Michael Ashby

THE GOLF COURSE IN THE SKY

As eighteen flags flew at half mast, and
Glasses were soberly raised high
The latest member was having a ball
At the golf course in the sky

Freed from the gravity of the situation
The first tee shot soared through space
Bringing a wondrous, beaming smile
To a kind, down to earth face

Surrounded by old club friends
Once thought never to be seen again
The infinity course beckoned ahead
Eighteen holes were for mere mortal men

Michael Ashby

Public Comments from my facebook page:

Emma Kay Wallace *I know a man that this fits to a tee.*

Cindy Pittman *Watch how far you drive that ball Marvin. I Love You and I miss hearing how much you beat Scott at golf.*

Kathy Brooks *Just lovely....wish I'd seen this years ago when we lost my Dad.*

Beth Bridgwater *Love this I shared it. Tim would have liked this.*

Annette Marek Church *In loving memory of my brother-in-law(Steve) who passed away 4wks ago.*

THE PASSING OF A FOOTBALLER

Football's a match made in heaven
Which is fan-tastic news for me
And heaven's a level playing field
Where anyone can kick off for free

The referee needs no introduction
Or whistle for a foul blow
When God raises his eyebrows
None argue with the penalty or throw

The transfer window never closes
As new players arrive all the time
There's always a top team to play on
As for the kit, I just wish I'd brought mine

We kick off side by side in a minute
Cheered by old family, teammates and friends
Football's really a blast in heaven
After your first whistle the matches never end

Michael Ashby

THE RUGBY PLAYER'S LAST TRY

The rugby ball inside the coffin
Rather gave the game away
As a diehard rugby warrior
Determined to play on in future days

Believing there was more than one H in heaven
At the ends of astral turf grounds
And that the rugby universe cup
Was still in its early rounds

After a lifetime that had seemed eighty minutes
With a body clock now in the red
The gladiator scored his last mortal try
Touching his head down on mother earth's bed

Michael Ashby

TRUE LOVE NEVER DIES

True love lay within
Beating Taj Mahal hearts; stilled
Their love warms the world

Michael Ashby

WE ARE NOT GONE

We are not gone
While you cry with us
We are not gone
While you smile with us
We are not gone
While you remember with us

We will come
When you call our names
We will come
When we feel your pain
We will come
On your final day

It could never be
That we
Would never be

We shall always
Be together
Forever

WE ARE NOT GONE

Michael Ashby

YOUR GREATEST TEST

Until the question..... is asked of you
Your answer..... is unknown
And for your longest..... days and nights
You will feel..... so, so alone

But with your..... indomitable lifeforce
And your subconscious..... will to survive
You will
You will pass..... your greatest test

And feel yourself slowly come alive

Michael Ashby

888,246

Carefully the elephant crossed the room
Carpeted with 888,246 poppies
Not one poppy was hurt
A poppy is never forgotten

Michael Ashby

(Blood Swept Lands and Seas of Red at The Tower Of London.)

LONG ESTABLISHED FUNERAL POEMS

"Funeral poems that resonate with me, and also poems of exquisite beauty that celebrate the joy of the human spirit are included here.

When mother nature and father time bequeathed mankind with a built-in self destruct button, they challenged the writers of the world to express their feelings on death."

Michael Ashby

EVERYTHING PASSES AND VANISHES

Everything passes and vanishes;
Everything leaves its trace;
And often you see in a footstep
What you could not see in a face.

William Allingham

FOUR DUCKS ON A POND

Four ducks on a pond,
A grass-bank beyond,
A blue sky of spring,
White clouds on the wing;
What a little thing
To remember for years -
To remember with tears!

William Allingham

TO MY DEAR AND LOVING HUSBAND

If ever two were one, then surely we.
If ever man were loved by wife, then thee;
If ever wife was happy in a man,
Compare with me ye women if you can.
I prize thy love more than whole mines of gold,
Or all the riches that the East doth hold.
My love is such that rivers cannot quench,
Nor ought but love from thee give recompense.
Thy love is such I can no way repay;
The heavens reward thee manifold, I pray.
Then while we live, in love let's so persever,
That when we live no more, we may live ever.

Anne Bradstreet

THE SHIP

What is dying
I am standing on the seashore, a ship sails in the morning breeze and starts for the ocean.
She is an object of beauty and I stand watching her till at last she fades on the horizon and someone at my side says: "She is gone."
Gone!
Where
Gone from my sight that is all.
She is just as large in the masts, hull and spars as she was when I saw her, and just as able to bear her load of living freight to its destination.
The diminished size and total loss of sight is in me, not in her, and just at the moment when someone at my side says,
"She is gone"
there are others who are watching her coming, and other voices take up a glad shout:
"There she comes!"
and that is dying.

Bishop Brent

THE OLD STOIC

Riches I hold in light esteem
And Love I laugh to scorn
The Lust of Fame was but a dream
That vanished with the morn –

And if I pray – the only prayer
That moves my lips for me
Is – 'Leave the heart that now I bear
And give me liberty.'

Yes, as my swift days near their goal
'Tis all that I implore –
In life and death, a chainless soul
With courage to endure!

Emily Bronte

THE SOLDIER

If I should die, think only this of me:
  That there's some corner of a foreign field
That is for ever England. There shall be
  In that rich earth a richer dust concealed;
A dust whom England bore, shaped, made aware,
  Gave, once, her flowers to love, her ways to roam,
A body of England's, breathing English air,
  Washed by the rivers, blest by suns of home.

And think, this heart, all evil shed away,
  A pulse in the eternal mind, no less
  Gives somewhere back the thoughts by England given;
Her sights and sounds; dreams happy as her day;
  And laughter, learnt of friends; and gentleness,
  In hearts at peace, under an English heaven.

Rupert Brooke

THOW DO I LOVE THEE? LET ME COUNT THE WAYS (SONNET FROM THE PORTUGUESE No. 43)

How do I love thee? Let me count the ways.
I love thee to the depth and breadth and height
My soul can reach, when feeling out of sight
For the ends of Being and ideal Grace.
I love thee to the level of everyday's
Most quiet need, by sun and candle-light.
I love thee freely, as men strive for Right;
I love thee purely, as they turn from Praise.
I love thee with the passion put to use
In my old griefs, and with my childhood's faith.
I love thee with a love I seemed to lose
With my lost saints - I love thee with the breath,
Smiles, tears, of all my life! - and, if God choose,
I shall but love thee better after death.

Elizabeth Barrett Browning

HOME- THOUGHTS, FROM ABROAD ("O TO BE IN ENGLAND")

O to be in England
Now that April's there,
And whoever wakes in England
Sees, some morning, unaware,
That the loweet boughs and the brushwood sheaf
Round the elm-tree bole are in tiny leaf,
While the chaffinch sings on the orchard bough
In England-now!

And after April, when May follows,
And the whitethroat builds, and all the swallows!
Hark, where my blossomed pear-tree in the hedge
Leans to the field and scatters on the clover
Blossoms and dewdrops-at the bent spray's edge-
That's the wise thrush: he sings each song twice
over,
Lest you should think he never could recapture
The first fine careless rapture!
And though the fields look rough with hoary dew,
All will be gay when noontide wakes anew
The buttercups, the little children's dower
-Far brighter than this gaudy melon-flower!

Robert Browning

EPITAPH ON A FRIEND

An honest man here lies at rest,
The friend of man, the friend of truth,
The friend of age, the guide of youth;
Few hearts like his, with virtue warm'd,
Few heads with knowledge so inform'd;
If there's another world, he lives in bliss;
If there is none, he made the best of this.

Robbie Burns

SHE WALKS IN BEAUTY

She walks in beauty, like the night
   Of cloudless climes and starry skies;
And all that's best of dark and bright
   Meet in her aspect and her eyes:
Thus mellowed to that tender light
   Which heaven to gaudy day denies.

One shade the more, one ray the less,
   Had half impaired the nameless grace
Which waves in every raven tress,
   Or softly lightens o'er her face;
Where thoughts serenely sweet express
   How pure, how dear their dwelling place.

And on that cheek, and o'er that brow,
   So soft, so calm, yet eloquent,
The smiles that win, the tints that glow,
   But tell of days in goodness spent,
A mind at peace with all below,
   A heart whose love is innocent!

Lord Byron

SO, WE'LL GO NO MORE A ROVING

So, we'll go no more a roving
So late into the night,
Though the heart be still as loving,
And the moon be still as bright.

For the sword outwears its sheath,
And the soul wears out the breast,
And the heart must pause to breathe,
And love itself have rest.

Though the night was made for loving,
And the day returns too soon,
Yet we'll go no more a roving
By the light of the moon.

Lord Byron

A KNIGHT'S TOMB

Where is the grave of Sir Arthur O'Kellyn?
Where may the grave of that good man be?
By the side of a spring, on the breast of Helvellyn,
Under the twigs of a young birch tree!
The oak that in summer was sweet to hear,
And rustled its leaves in the fall of the year,
And whistled and roared in the winter alone,
Is gone, and the birch in its stead is grown.
The Knight's bones are dust,
And his good sword rust;
His soul is with the saints, I trust.

Samuel Taylor Coleridge

LEISURE (WHAT IS THIS LIFE IF FULL OF CARE)

What is this life if, full of care,
We have no time to stand and stare.

No time to stand beneath the boughs
And stare as long as sheep or cows.

No time to see, when woods we pass,
Where squirrels hide their nuts in grass.

No time to see, in broad daylight,
Streams full of stars, like skies at night.

No time to turn at Beauty's glance,
And watch her feet, how they can dance.

No time to wait, till her mouth can
Enrich that smile her eyes began.

A poor life this if, full of care,
We have no time to stand and stare.

William Henry Davies

A COFFIN IS A SMALL DOMAIN

A Coffin - is a small Domain,
Yet able to contain
A Citizen of Paradise
In it diminished Plane.

A Grave - is a restricted Breadth -
Yet ampler than the Sun -
And all the Seas He populates
And Lands He looks upon

To Him who on its small Repose
Bestows a single Friend -
Circumference without Relief -
Or Estimate - or End -

Emily Dickinson

A CLOUD WITHDREW FOM THE SKY

A Cloud withdrew from the Sky
Superior Glory be
But that Cloud and its Auxiliaries
Are forever lost to me

Had I but further scanned
Had I secured the Glow
In an Hermetic Memory
It had availed me now,

Never to pass the Angel
With a glance and a Bow
Till I am firm in Heaven
Is my intention now.

Emily Dickinson

AFTER GREAT PAIN, A FORMAL FEELING COMES

After great pain, a formal feeling comes -
The Nerves sit ceremonious, like Tombs -
And stiff Heart questions was it He, that bore,
And Yesterday, or Centuries before?

The Feet, mechanical, go round -
Of Ground, or Air, or Ought -
A Wooden way
Regardless grown,
A Quartz contentment, like a stone -

This is the Hour of Lead -
Remembered, if outlived,
As Freezing persons, recollect the Snow -
First – Chill – then Stupor – then the letting go -

Emily Dickinson

BECAUSE I COULD NOT STOP FOR DEATH

Because I could not stop for Death,
He kindly stopped for me;
The carriage held but just ourselves
And Immortality.

We slowly drove, he knew no haste,
And I had put away
My labor, and my leisure too,
For His civility.

We passed the school, where children strove
At recess, in the ring;
We passed the fields of gazing grain,
We passed the setting sun.

Or rather, he passed us;
The dews drew quivering and chill,
For only gossamer my gown,
My tippet only tulle.

We paused before a house that seemed
A swelling of the ground;
The roof was scarcely visibile,
The cornice but a mound.

Since then 'tis centuries, and yet each
Feels shorter than the the day
I first surmised the horses' heads
Were towards eternity.

Emily Dickinson

IF I CAN STOP ONE HEART FROM BREAKING

If I can stop one heart from breaking,
I shall not live in vain;
If I can ease one life the aching,
Or cool one pain,
Or help one fainting robin
Unto his nest again,
I shall not live in vain.

Emily Dickinson

I SHALL KNOW WHY - WHEN TIME IS OVER

I shall know why, when Time is over,
And I have ceased to wonder why;
Christ will explain each separate anguish
In the fair schoolroom of the sky.
He will tell me what Peter promised,
And I, for wonder at his woe,
I shall forget the drop of Anguish
That scalds me now, that scalds me now.

Emily Dickinson

PARTING

My life closed twice before its close-
It yet remains to see
If Immortality unveil
A third event to me

So huge, so hopeless to conceive
As these that twice befell.
Parting is all we know of heaven,
And all we need of hell.

Emily Dickinson

DEATH BE NOT PROUD

Death be not proud, though some have called thee
Mighty and dreadfull, for, thou art not soe,
For, those, whom thou think'st, thou dost overthrow,
Die not, poore death, nor yet canst thou kill mee;
From rest and sleepe, which but thy pictures bee,
Much pleasure, then from thee, much more must flow,
And soonest our best men with thee doe go,
Rest of their bones, and soules deliverie.
Thou art slave to Fate, chance, kings, and desperate men,
And dost with poyson, warre, and sicknesse dwell,
And poppie, or charmes can make us sleepe as well,
And better than thy stroake; why swell'st thou then?
One short sleepe past, wee wake eternally,
And death shall be no more, Death, thou shalt die.

John Donne

DO NOT STAND AT MY GRAVE & WEEP

Do not stand at my grave and weep,
I am not there, I do not sleep.
I am in a thousand winds that blow,
I am the softly falling snow.
I am the gentle showers of rain,
I am the fields of ripening grain.
I am in the morning hush,
I am in the graceful rush
Of beautiful birds in circling flight,
I am the starshine of the night.
I am in the flowers that bloom,
I am in a quiet room.
I am in the birds that sing,
I am in each lovely thing.
Do not stand at my grave bereft
I am not there. I have not left.

Mary Elizabeth Frye

DEATH

Then Almitra spoke, saying, "We would ask now of Death."
And he said:
You would know the secret of death.
But how shall you find it unless you seek it in the heart of life
The owl whose night-bound eyes are blind unto the day cannot unveil the mystery of light.
If you would indeed behold the spirit of death, open your heart wide unto the body of life.
For life and death are one, even as the river and the sea are one.
In the depth of your hopes and desires lies your silent knowledge of the beyond;
And like seeds dreaming beneath the snow your heart dreams of spring.
Trust the dreams, for in them is hidden the gate to eternity.
Your fear of death is but the trembling of the shepherd when he stands before the king whose hand is to be laid upon him in honour.
Is the shepherd not joyful beneath his trembling, that he shall wear the mark of the king
Yet is he not more mindful of his trembling
For what is it to die but to stand naked in the wind and to melt into the sun
And what is to cease breathing, but to free the breath from its restless tides, that it may rise and expand and seek God unencumbered

Only when you drink from the river of silence
shall you indeed sing.
And when you have reached the mountain top,
then you shall begin to climb.
And when the earth shall claim your limbs, then
shall you truly dance.

Khalil Gibran

JOY AND SORROW

Then a woman said, "Speak to us of Joy and Sorrow."
And he answered:
Your joy is your sorrow unmasked.
And the selfsame well from which your laughter rises was oftentimes filled with your tears.
And how else can it be
The deeper that sorrow carves into your being, the more joy you can contain.
Is not the cup that hold your wine the very cup that was burned in the potter's oven
And is not the lute that soothes your spirit, the very wood that was hollowed with knives
When you are joyous, look deep into your heart and you shall find it is only that which has given you sorrow that is giving you joy.
When you are sorrowful look again in your heart, and you shall see that in truth you are weeping for that which has been your delight.
Some of you say, "Joy is greater than sorrow," and others say, "Nay, sorrow is the greater."
But I say unto you, they are inseparable.
Together they come, and when one sits alone with you at your board, remember that the other is asleep upon your bed.
Verily you are suspended like scales between your sorrow and your joy.
Only when you are empty are you at standstill and balanced.
When the treasure-keeper lifts you to weigh his gold and his silver, needs must your joy or your sorrow rise or fall.
Khalil Gibran

ELEGY WRITTEN IN A COUNTRY CHURCHYARD

The curfew tolls the knell of parting day,
The lowing herd wind slowly o'er the lea
The plowman homeward plods his weary way,
And leaves the world to darkness and to me.

Now fades the glimmering landscape on the sight,
And all the air a solemn stillness holds,
Save where the beetle wheels his droning flight,
And drowsy tinklings lull the distant folds;

Save that from yonder ivy-mantled tower
The moping owl does to the moon complain
Of such as, wandering near her secret bower,
Molest her ancient solitary reign.

Beneath those rugged elms, that yew-tree's shade,
Where heaves the turf in many a mouldering heap,
Each in his narrow cell for ever laid,
The rude forefathers of the hamlet sleep.

The breezy call of incense-breathing morn,
The swallow twittering from the straw-built shed,
The cock's shrill clarion or the echoing horn,
No more shall rouse them from their lowly bed.

For them no more the blazing hearth shall burn,
Or busy housewife ply her evening care:
No children run to lisp their sire's return,
Or climb his knees the envied kiss to share.

Oft did the harvest to their sickle yield,
Their furrow oft the stubborn glebe has broke;
How jocund did they drive their team afield!
How bowed the woods beneath their sturdy stroke!

Let not Ambition mock their useful toil,
Their homely joys and destiny obscure;
Nor Grandeur hear, with a disdainful smile
The short and simple annals of the poor.

The boast of heraldry, the pomp of power,
And all that beauty, all that wealth e'er gave,
Awaits alike the inevitable hour.
The paths of glory lead but to the grave.

Nor you, ye Proud, impute to these the fault,
If Memory o'er their tomb no trophies raise,
Where through the long-drawn aisle and fretted vault
The pealing anthem swells the note of praise.

Can storied urn or animated bust
Back to its mansion call the fleeting breath?
Can Honour's voice provoke the silent dust,
Or Flattery soothe the dull cold ear of Death?

Perhaps in this neglected spot is laid
Some heart once pregnant with celestial fire;
Hands, that the rod of empire might have swayed,
Or waked to ecstasy the living lyre.

But Knowledge to their eyes her ample page
Rich with the spoils of time did ne'er unroll;
Chill Penury repressed their noble rage,

And froze the genial current of the soul.

Full many a gem of purest ray serene,
The dark unfathom'd caves of ocean bear:
Full many a flower is born to blush unseen,
And waste its sweetness on the desert air.

Some village-Hampden, that with dauntless breast
The little tyrant of his fields withstood;
Some mute inglorious Milton here may rest,
Some Cromwell guiltless of his country's blood.

The applause of listening senates to command,
The threats of pain and ruin to despise,
To scatter plenty o'er a smiling land,
And read their history in a nation's eyes,

Their lot forbade: nor circumscribed alone
Their growing virtues, but their crimes confined;
Forbade to wade through slaughter to a throne,
And shut the gates of mercy on mankind,

The struggling pangs of conscious truth to hide,
To quench the blushes of ingenuous shame,
Or heap the shrine of Luxury and Pride
With incense kindled at the Muse's flame.

Far from the madding crowd's ignoble strife,
Their sober wishes never learned to stray;
Along the cool sequestered vale of life
They kept the noiseless tenor of their way.

Yet even these bones from insult to protect,

Some frail memorial still erected nigh,
With uncouth rhymes and shapeless sculpture decked,
Implores the passing tribute of a sigh.

Their name, their years, spelt by the unlettered muse,
The place of fame and elegy supply:
And many a holy text around she strews,
That teach the rustic moralist to die.

For who to dumb Forgetfulness a prey,
This pleasing anxious being e'er resign'd,
Left the warm precincts of the cheerful day,
Nor cast one longing, lingering look behind?

On some fond breast the parting soul relies,
Some pious drops the closing eye requires;
Even from the tomb the voice of Nature cries,
Even in our ashes live their wonted fires.

For thee, who mindful of the unhonoured Dead
Dost in these lines their artless tale relate;
If chance, by lonely Contemplation led,
Some kindred spirit shall inquire thy fate,

Haply some hoary-headed swain may say,
"Oft have we seen him at the peep of dawn
Brushing with hasty steps the dews away
To meet the sun upon the upland lawn.

"There at the foot of yonder nodding beech
That wreathes its old fantastic roots so high,
His listless length at noontide would he stretch,

And pore upon the brook that babbles by.

"Hard by yon wood, now smiling as in scorn,
Muttering his wayward fancies he would rove,
Now drooping, woeful wan, like one forlorn,
Or crazed with care, or crossed in hopeless love.

"One morn I missed him on the customed hill,
Along the heath and near his favourite tree;
Another came; nor yet beside the rill,
Nor up the lawn, nor at the wood was he;

"The next with dirges due in sad array
Slow through the church-way path we saw him borne.
Approach and read (for thou canst read) the lay,
Grav'd on the stone beneath yon aged thorn."

THE EPITAPH Here rests his head upon the lap of EarthA youth to Fortune and to Fame unknown.Fair Science frowned not on his humble birth,And Melancholy marked him for her own. Large was his bounty, and his soul sincere,Heaven did a recompense as largely send:He gave to Misery all he had, a tear,He gained from Heaven ('twas all he wished) a friend. No farther seek his merits to disclose,Or draw his frailties from their dread abode,(There they alike in trembling hope repose)The bosom of his Father and his God.

Thomas Gray

EPITAPH ON A CHILD

Here, freed from pain, secure from misery, lies
A child, the darling of his parents' eyes;
A gentler lamb ne'er sported on the plain,
A fairer flower will never bloom again.
Few were the days allotted to his breath;
Now let him sleep in peace his night of death.

Thomas Gray

LIFE

I made a posie, while the day ran by:
Here will I smell my remnant out, and tie
My life within this band.
But Time did beckon to the flowers, and they
By noon most cunningly did steal away,
And withered in my hand.

My hand was next to them, and then my heart:
I took, without more thinking, in good part
Time's gentle admonition;
Who did so sweetly death's sad taste convey,
Making my mind to smell my fatal day;
Yet sugaring the suspicion.

Farewell dear flowers, sweetly your time ye spent,
Fit, while ye lived, for smell or ornament,
And after death for cures,
I follow straight without complaints or grief,
Since if my scent be good, I care not if
It be as short as yours.

George Herbert

TO DAFFODILS

Fair daffodils, we weep to see
You haste away so soon:
As yet the early-rising sun
Has not attained his noon
Stay, stay,
Until the hasting day
Has run
But to the evensong;
And, having prayed together, we
Will go with you along.

We have short time to stay as you;
We have as short as spring;
As quick a growth to meet decay,
As you or anything.
We die,
As your hours do, and dry
Away
Like to the summer's rain;
Or as the pearls of morning's dew,
Ne'er to be found again.

Robert Herrick

UPON A CHILD THAT DIED

Here she lies, a pretty bud
Lately made of flesh and blood,
Who as soon fell fast asleep
As her little eyes did peep.
Give her strewings, but not stir
The earth that lightly covers her.

Robert Herrick

DEATH IS NOTHING AT ALL

Death is nothing at all.
It does not count.
I have only slipped away into the next room.
Nothing has happened.
Everything remains exactly as it was.
I am I, and you are you, and the old life that we lived so fondly together is untouched, unchanged.
Whatever we were to each other, that we are still.
Call me by the old familiar name.
Speak of me in the easy way which you always used.
Put no difference into your tone.
Wear no forced air of solemnity or sorrow.
Laugh as we always laughed at the little jokes that we enjoyed together. Play, smile, think of me, pray for me.
Let my name be ever the household word that it always was.
Let it be spoken without an effort, without the ghost of a shadow upon it. Life means all that it ever meant.
It is the same as it ever was.
There is absolute and unbroken continuity.
What is this death but a negligible accident
Why should I be out of mind because I am out of sight
I am but waiting for you, for an interval, somewhere very near, just round the corner.
All is well.
Nothing is hurt; nothing is lost.
One brief moment and all will be as it was before.
How we shall laugh at the trouble of parting when we meet again!

Henry Scott Holland

ON MY FIRST SONNE

Farewell, thou child of my right hand, and joy;
My sinne was too much hope of thee, lov'd boy,
Seven yeeres tho'wert lent to me, and I thee pay,
Exacted by thy fate, on the just day.
O, could I lose all father, now. For why
Will man lament the state he should envie?
To have so soone scap'd worlds, and fleshes rage,
And, if no other miserie, yet age?
Rest in soft peace, and, ask'd, say here doth lye
BEN. JONSON his best piece of poetrie.
For whose sake, henceforth, all his vowes be such,
As what he loves may never like too much.

Ben Jonson

BRIGHT STAR

Bright Star! would I were steadfast as thou art -
Not in lone splendour hung aloft the night,
And watching, with eternal lids apart,
Like Nature's patient sleepless Eremite,
The moving waters at their priestlike task
Of pure ablution round earth's human shores,
Or gazing on the new soft fallen mask
Of snow upon the mountains and the moors -
No - yet still steadfast, still unchangeable,
Pillow'd upon my fair love's ripening breast
To feel for ever its soft fall and swell,
Awake for ever in a sweet unrest;
Still, still to hear her tender-taken breath,
And so live ever - or else swoon to death

John Keats

ENDYMION

A thing of beauty is a joy for ever:
Its loveliness increases; it will never
Pass into nothingness; but still will keep
A bower quiet for us, and a sleep
Full of sweet dreams, and health, and quiet breathing.
Therefore, on every morrow, are we wreathing
A flowery band to bind us to the earth,
Spite of despondence, of the inhuman dearth
Of noble natures, of the gloomy days,
Of all the unhealthy and o'er-darkened ways
Made for our searching: yes, in spite of all,
Some shape of beauty moves away the pall
From our dark spirits. Such the sun, the moon,
Trees old, and young, sprouting a shady boon
For simple sheep; and such are daffodils
With the green world they live in; and clear rills
That for themselves a cooling covert make
'Gainst the hot season; the mid-forest brake,
Rich with a sprinkling of fair musk-rose blooms:
And such too is the grandeur of the dooms
We have imagined for the mighty dead;
All lovely tales that we have heard or read:
An endless fountain of immortal drink,
Pouring unto us from the heaven's brink.

John Keats

HIS LAST SONNET

Bright star, would I were steadfast as thou art! -
Not in lone splendour hung aloft the night,
And watching, with eternal lids apart,
Like Nature's patient sleepless Eremite,
The moving waters at their priestlike task
Of pure ablution round earth's human shores,
Or gazing on the new soft fallen mask
Of snow upon the mountains and the moors -
No -yet still steadfast, still unchangeable,
Pillowed upon my fair love's ripening breast,
To feel for ever its soft fall and swell,
Awake for ever in a sweet unrest,
Still, still to hear her tender-taken breath,
And so live ever -or else swoon to death.

John Keats

TO SLEEP

O soft embalmer of the still midnight!
Shutting, with careful fingers and benign,
Our gloom-pleased eyes, embowered from the light,
Enshaded in forgetfulness divine;
O soothest Sleep! if so it please thee, close,
In midst of this thine hymn, my willing eyes,
Or wait the amen, ere thy poppy throws
Around my bed its lulling charities;
Then save me, or the passed day will shine
Upon my pillow, breeding many woes;
Save me from curious conscience, that still lords
Its strength, for darkness burrowing like a mole;
Turn the key deftly in the oiled wards,
And seal the hushed casket of my soul.

John Keats

WHEN I HAVE FEARS THAT I MAY CEASE TO BE

When I have fears that I may cease to be
Before my pen has glean'd my teeming brain,
Before high piled books, in charactry,
Hold like rich garners the full ripen'd grain;
When I behold, upon the night's starr'd face,
Huge cloudy symbols of a high romance,
And think that I may never live to trace
Their shadows, with the magic hand of chance;
And when I feel, fair creature of an hour,
That I shall never look upon thee more,
Never have relish in the fairy power
Of unreflecting love;—then on the shore
Of the wide world I stand alone, and think
Till love and fame to nothingness do sink.

John Keats

A PSALM OF LIFE

Tell me not, in mournful numbers,
Life is but an empty dream!-
For the soul is dead that slumbers,
And things are not what they seem.
Life is real! Life is earnest!
And the grave is not its goal;
Dust thou art, to dust returnest,
Was not spoken of the soul.
Not enjoyment, and not sorrow,
Is our destined end or way;
But to act, that each to-morrow
Find us farther than to-day.
Art is long, and Time is fleeting,
And our hearts, though stout and brave,
Still, like muffled drums, are beating
Funeral marches to the grave.
In the world's broad field of battle,
In the bivouac of Life,
Be not like dumb, driven cattle!
Be a hero in the strife!
Trust no Future, howe'er pleasant!
Let the dead Past bury its dead!
Act,-act in the living Present!
Heart within, and God o'erhead!
Lives of great men all remind us
We can make our lives sublime,
And, departing, leave behind us
Footprints on the sands of time;
Footprints, that perhaps another, Sailing o'er life's

solemn main,
A forlorn and shipwrecked brother,
Seeing, shall take heart again.
Let us, then, be up and doing,
With a heart for any fate;
Still achieving, still pursuing,
Learn to labor and to wait

Henry Wadsworth Longfellow

THE CROSS OF SNOW

In the long, sleepless watches of the night,
A gentle face- the face of one long dead-
Looks at me from the wall, where round its head
The night-lamp casts a halo of pale light.
Here in this room she died; and soul more white
Never through martyrdom of fire was led
To its repose; nor can in books be read
The legend of a life more benedight.
There is a mountain in the distant West
That, sun-defying, in its deep ravines
Displays a cross of snow on its side.
Such is the cross I wear upon my breast
These eighteen years, through all the changing scenes
And seasons, changeless since the day she died.

Henry Wadsworth Longfellow

ON A FLY DRINKING OUT OF HIS CUP

Busy, curious, thirsty fly!
Drink with me and drink as I:
Freely welcome to my cup,
Couldst thou sip and sip it up:
Make the most of life you may,
Life is short and wears away.

Both alike are mine and thine
Hastening quick to their decline:
Thine's a summer, mine's no more,
Though repeated to threescore.
Threescore summers when they're gone,
Will appear as short as one!

William Oldys

A DIRGE

Why were you born when the snow was falling?
You should have come to the cuckoo's calling,
Or when grapes are green in the cluster,
Or, at least, when lithe swallows muster
For their far off flying
From summer dying.
Why did you die when the lambs were cropping?
You should have died at the apples' dropping,
When the grasshopper comes to trouble,
And the wheat-fields are sodden stubble,
And all winds go sighing
For sweet things dying.

Christina Georgina Rossetti

REMEMBER

Remember me when I am gone away,
Gone far away into the silent land;
When you can no more hold me by the hand,
Nor I half turn to go yet turning stay.
Remember me when no more day by day
You tell me of our future that you planned:
Only remember me; you understand
It will be late to counsel then or pray.
Yet if you should forget me for a while
And afterwards remember, do not grieve:
For if the darkness and corruption leave
A vestige of the thoughts that once I had,
Better by far you should forget and smile
Than that you should remember and be sad.

Christina Georgina Rossetti

THE FIRST SPRING DAY

I wonder if the sap is stirring yet,
If wintry birds are dreaming of a mate,
If frozen snowdrops feel as yet the sun
And crocus fires are kindling one by one:
    Sing, robin, sing:
I still am sore in doubt concerning Spring.

I wonder if the springtide of this year
Will bring another Spring both lost and dear;
If heart and spirit will find out their Spring,
Or if the world alone will bud and sing:
    Sing, hope, to me;
Sweet notes, my hope, soft notes for memory.

The sap will surely quicken soon or late,
The tardiest bird will twitter to a mate;
So Spring must dawn again with warmth and bloom,
Or in this world, or in the world to come:
    Sing, voice of Spring,
Till I too blossom and rejoice and sing.

Christina Georgina Rossetti

UPHILL

Does the road wind up-hill all the way?
Yes, to the very end.
Will the day's journey take the whole long day?
From morn to night my friend.

But is there for the night a resting-place?
A roof for when the slow dark hours begin.
May not the darkness hide it from my face?
You cannot miss that inn.

Shall I meet other wayfarers at night?
Those who have gone before.
Then must I knock, or call when just in sight?
They will not keep you standing at that door.

Shall I find comfort, travel-sore and weak?
Of labour, you shall find the sum.
Will there be beds for me and all who seek?
Yea, beds for all who come.

Christina Georgina Rossetti

WHEN I AM DEAD, MY DEAREST

When I am dead, my dearest
        Sing no sad songs for me;
Plant thou no roses at my head,
        Nor shady cypress tree:
Be the green grass above me
        With showers and dewdrops wet;
And if thou wilt, remember,
        And if thou wilt, forget.

I shall not see the shadows,
        I shall not feel the rain;
I shall not hear the nightingale
        Sing on, as if in pain:
And dreaming through the twilight
        That doth not rise nor set,
Haply I may remember,
        And haply may forget.

Christina Georgina Rossetti

ALL THE WORLD'S A STAGE

All the world's a stage,
And all the men and women merely players;
They have their exits and their entrances;
And one man in his time plays many parts,
His acts being seven ages. At first the infant,
Mewling and puking in the nurse's arms;
And then the whining school-boy, with his satchel
And shining morning face, creeping like snail
Unwillingly to school. And then the lover,
Sighing like furnace, with a woeful ballad
Made to his mistress' eyebrow. Then a soldier,
Full of strange oaths, and bearded like the pard,
Jealous in honour, sudden and quick in quarrel,
Seeking the bubble reputation
Even in the cannon's mouth. And then the justice,
In fair round belly with good capon lin'd,
With eyes severe and beard of formal cut,
Full of wise saws and modern instances;
And so he plays his part. The sixth age shifts
Into the lean and slipper'd pantaloon,
With spectacles on nose and pouch on side;
His youthful hose, well sav'd, a world too wide
For his shrunk shank; and his big manly voice,
Turning again toward childish treble, pipes
And whistles in his sound. Last scene of all,
That ends this strange eventful history,
Is second childishness and mere oblivion;
Sans teeth, sans eyes, sans taste, sans everything.
William Shakespeare

AYE, BUT TO DIE, AND GO WE KNOW NOT WHERE

Aye, but to die ,and go we know not where;
To lie in cold obstruction and to rot;
This sensible warm motion to become
A kneaded clod; and the delighted spirit
To bathe in fiery floods, or to reside
In thrilling region of thick-ribbed ice;
To be imprison'd in the viewless winds,
And blown with restless violence round about
The pendant world ; or to be worse than worst
Of those that lawless and incertain thoughts
Imagine howling: 'tis too horrible!
The weariest and most loathed wordly life
That age, ache, penury and imprisonment
Can lay on nature is a paradise
To what we fear of death.

William Shakespeare

COWARDS

Cowards die many times before their deaths:
The valiant never taste of death but once.
of all the wonders that I yet have heard,
It seems to me most strange that men should fear;
Seeing that death, a necessary end,
Will come, when it will come.

William Shakespeare

FIDELE'S DIRGE

Fear no more the heat o' the sun
Nor the furious winter's rages;
Thou thy worldly task hast done,
Home art gone and ta'en thy wages:
Golden lads and girls all must,
As chimney-sweepers, come to dust.

Fear no more the frown o' the great,
Thou art past the tyrant's stroke;
Care no more to clothe and eat;
To thee the reed is as the oak:
The sceptre, learning, physic, must
All follow this, and come to dust.

Fear no more the lightning-flash
Nor the all-dreaded thunder-stone;
Fear not slander, censure rash;
Thou hast finish'd joy and moan:
All lovers young, all lovers must
Consign to thee, and come to dust.

No exorciser harm thee!
Nor no witchcraft charm thee!
Ghost unlaid forbear thee!
Nothing ill come near thee!
Quiet consummation have;
And renowned be thy grave!

William Shakespeare

OUR REVELS NOW ARE ENDED

Our revels now are ended. These our actors,
As I foretold you, were all spirits and
Are melted into air, into thin air;
And, like the baseless fabric of this vision,
The cloud-capped tow'rs, the gorgeous palaces,
The solemn temples, the great globe itself,
Yea, all which it inherit, shall dissolve,
And, like this insubstantial pageant faded,
Leave not a rack behind. We are such stuff
As dreams are made on, and our little life
Is rounded with a sleep.

William Shakespeare

SHALL I COMPARE THEE TO A SUMMER'S DAY

Shall I compare thee to a summer's day?
Thou art more lovely and more temperate:
Rough winds do shake the darling buds of May,
And summer's lease hath all too short a date:
Sometime too hot the eye of heaven shines,
And often is his gold complexion dimm'd,
And every fair from fair sometime declines,
By chance or natures changing course untrimm'd:
But thy eternal summer shall not fade,
Nor lose possession of that fair thou owest,
Nor shall death brag thou wandrest in his shade,
When in eternal lines to time thou growest,
So long as men can breathe or eyes can see
So long lives this, and this gives life to thee.

William Shakespeare

SONNET 29

When, in disgrace with fortune and men's eyes,
I all alone beweep my outcast state,
And trouble deaf heaven with my bootless cries,
And look upon myself, and curse my fate,
Wishing me like to one more rich in hope,
Featured like him, like him with friends possessed,
Desiring this man's art, and that man's scope,
With what I most enjoy contented least;
Yet in these thoughts myself almost despising,
Haply I think on thee – and then my state,
Like to the lark at break of day arising
From sullen earth, sings hymns at heaven's gate;
For thy sweet love rememb'red such wealth brings
That then I scorn to change my state with kings.

William Shakespeare

SONNET 30

When to the sessions of sweet silent thought
I summon up remembrance of things past,
I sigh the lack of many a thing I sought,
And with old woes new wail my dear time's waste;
Then can I drown an eye, unused to flow,
For precious friends hid in death's dateless night,
And weep afresh love's long since cancelled woe,
And moan th'expense of many a vanished sight;
Then can I grieve at grievances foregone,
And heavily from woe to woe tell o'er
The sad account of fore -bemoaned moan,
Which I new pay as if not paid before.
But if the while I think on thee, dear friend,
All losses are restored and sorrows end.

William Shakespeare

SONNET 55

Not marble, nor the gilded monuments
Of princes, shall outlive this powerful rhyme;
But you shall shine more bright in these contents
Than unswept stone, besmeared with sluttish time.
When wasteful war shall statues overturn,
And broils root out the work of masonry,
Nor Mars his sword nor war's quick fire shall burn
The living record of your memory.
'Gainst death and all-oblivious enmity
Shall you pace forth; your praise shall still find room
Even in the eyes of all posterity
That wear this world out to the ending doom.
So, till the judgment that yourself arise,
You live in this, and dwell in lovers' eyes.

William Shakespeare

SONNET 60

Like as the waves make towards the pebbled shore,
So do our minutes hasten to their end;
Each changing place with that which goes before,
In sequent toil all forwards do contend.
Nativity, once in the main of light,
Crawls to maturity, wherewith being crown'd,
Crooked eclipses 'gainst his glory fight,
And Time that gave doth now his gift confound.
Time doth transfix the flourish set on youth
And delves the parallels in beauty's brow,
Feeds on the rarities of nature's truth,
And nothing stands but for his scythe to mow:
And yet to times in hope, my verse shall stand.
Praising thy worth, despite his cruel hand.

William Shakespeare

SONNET 116

Let me not to the marriage of true minds
Admit impediments. Love is not love
Which alters when it alteration finds,
Or bends with the remover to remove:
Oh, no! it is an ever fixed mark,
That looks on tempests and is never shaken;
It is the star to every wandering bark,
Whose worth's unknown, although his height be taken.
Love's not Time's fool, though rosy lips and cheeks
Within his bending sickle's compass come;
Love alters not with his brief hours and weeks,
But bears it out even to the edge of doom.
If this be error and upon me proved,
I never writ, nor no man ever loved.

William Shakespeare

TOMORROW, AND TOMORROW, AND TOMORROW

Tomorrow, and tomorrow, and tomorrow,
Creeps in this petty pace from day to day,
To the last syllable of recorded time;
And all our yesterdays have lighted fools
The way to dusty death. Out, out, brief candle!
Life's but a walking shadow, a poor player
That struts and frets his hour upon the stage
And then is heard no more: it is a tale
Told by an idiot, full of sound and fury,
Signifying nothing.

William Shakespeare

WHERE THE BEE SUCKS, THERE SUCK I

Where the bee sucks, there suck I:
In a cowslip's bell I lie;
There I couch when owls do cry.
On the bat's back I do fly
After summer merrily.
Merrily, merrily shall I live now
Under the blossom that hangs on the bough.

William Shakespeare

A LAMENT

O World ! O Life ! O Time !
On whose last steps I climb,
Trembling at that where I had stood before;
When will return the glory of your prime?
No more--Oh, never more!

Out of the day and night
A joy has taken flight;
Fresh spring, and summer, and winter hoar
Move my faint heart with grief, but with delight
No more--Oh, never more !

Percy Bysshe Shelley

MUSIC, WHEN SOFT VOICES DIE

Music, when soft voices die,
Vibrates in the memory -
Odours, when sweet violets sicken,
Live within the sense they quicken.

Rose leaves, when the rose is dead,
Are heap'd for the beloved's bed;
And so thy thoughts ,when thou art gone,
Love itself shall slumber on.

Percy Bysshe Shelley

MUTABILITY

We are as clouds that veil the midnight moon;
How restlessly they speed, and gleam, and quiver,
Streaking the darkness radiantly! – yet soon
Night closes round, and they are lost forever:

Or like forgotten lyres, whose dissonant strings
Give various response to each varying blast,
To whose frail frame no second motion brings
One mood or modulation like the last.

We rest. – A dream has power to poison sleep;
We rise. – One wandering thought pollutes the day;
We feel, conceive or reason, laugh or weep;
Embrace fond woe, or cast our cares away:

It is the same! – For, be it joy or sorrow,
The path of its departure still is free:
Man's yesterday may ne'er be like his morrow;
Nought may endure but Mutability.

Percy Bysshe Shelley

OZYMANDIAS

I met a traveller from an antique land
Who said: Two vast and trunkless legs of stone
Stand in the desert... Near them, on the sand,
Half sunk, a shatter'd visage lies, whose frown
And wrinkled lip and sneer of cold command,
Tell that its sculptor well those passions read
Which yet survive, stamp'd on these lifeless things,
The hand that mock'd them, and the heart that fed;
And on the pedestal these words appear:
'My name is Ozymandias, king of kings:
Look on my works, ye Mighty, and despair!'
Nothing beside remains. Round the decay
Of that colossal wreck, boundless and bare,
The lone and level sands stretch far away.

Percy Bysshe Shelley

TO JANE: THE KEEN STARS WERE TWINKLING

The keen stars were twinkling,
And the fair moon was rising among them,
Dear Jane!
The guitar was tinkling,
But the notes were not sweet till you sung them
Again.

As the moon's soft splendour
O'er the faint cold starlight of Heaven
Is thrown,
So your voice most tender
To the strings without soul had then given
Its own.

The stars will awaken,
Though the moon sleep a full hour later,
Tonight;
No leaf will be shaken
Whilst the dews of your melody scatter
Delight.

Though the sound overpowers,
Sing again, with your dear voice revealing
A tone
Of some world far from ours,
Where music and moonlight and feeling
Are one.

Percy Bysshe Shelley

ADONAIS (Final Words)

LIII.

Why linger, why turn back, why shrink, my Heart?
Thy hopes are gone before: from all things here
They have departed; thou shouldst now depart!
A light is passed from the revolving year,
And man, and woman; and what still is dear
Attracts to crush, repels to make thee wither.
The soft sky smiles, – the low wind whispers near:
'Tis Adonais calls! oh, hasten thither,
No more let Life divide what Death can join together.

LIV.

That Light whose smile kindles the Universe,
That Beauty in which all things work and move,
That Benediction which the eclipsing Curse
Of birth can quench not, that sustaining Love
Which through the web of being blindly wove
By man and beast and earth and air and sea,
Burns bright or dim, as each are mirrors of
The fire for which all thirst, now beams on me,
Consuming the last clouds of cold mortality.

LV.

The breath whose might I have invoked in song
Descends on me; my spirit's bark is driven
Far from the shore, far from the trembling throng
Whose sails were never to the tempest given;
The massy earth and sphered skies are riven!
I am borne darkly, fearfully, afar;
Whilst, burning through the inmost veil of Heaven,
The soul of Adonais, like a star,
Beacons from the abode where the Eternal are.

Alfred, Lord Tennyson

BREAK, BREAK, BREAK

Break, break, break,
On thy cold grey stones, O Sea!
And I would that my tongue could utter
The thoughts that arise in me.

O well for the fisherman's boy,
That he shouts with his sister at play!
O well for the sailor lad,
That he sings in his boat on the bay!

And the stately ships go on
To their haven under the hill!
But O for the touch of a vanish'd hand,
And the sound of a voice that is still!

Break, break, break,
At the foot of thy crags, O Sea!
But the tender grace of a day that is dead
Will never come back to me.

Alfred, Lord Tennyson

CROSSING THE BAR

Sunset and evening star,
And one clear call for me!
And may there be no moaning of the bar,
When I put out to sea,
But such a tide as moving seems asleep,
Too full for sound and foam,
When that which drew from out the boundless deep
Turns again home.
Twilight and evening bell,
And after that the dark!
And may there be no sadness of farewell,
When I embark;
For though from out our bourne of Time and Place
The flood may bear me far,
I hope to see my Pilot face to face
When I have crossed the bar.

Alfred, Lord Tennyson

IN MEMORIAM (Last Verses)

Whereof the man, that with me trod
This planet, was a noble type
Appearing ere the times were ripe,
That friend of mine who lives in God,

That God, which ever lives and loves,
One God, one law, one element,
And one far-off divine event,
To which the whole creation moves.

Alfred, Lord Tennyson

THERE IS A SOLEMN WIND TONIGHT

There is a solemn wind to-night
That sings of solemn rain;
The trees that have been quiet so long
Flutter and start again.
The slender trees, the heavy trees,
The fruit trees laden and proud,
Lift up their branches to the wind
That cries to them so loud.
The little bushes and the plants
Bow to the solemn sound,
And every tiniest blade of grass
Shakes on the quiet ground.

Alfred, Lord Tennyson

A SLUMBER DID MY SPIRIT SEAL

A slumber did my spirit seal;
I had no human fears:
She seemed a thing that could not feel
The touch of earthly years.

No motion has she now, no force:
She neither hears nor sees;
Rolled round in earth's diurnal course,
With rocks, and stones and trees.

William Wordsworth

COMPOSED UPON WESTMINSTER BRIDGE, SEPTEMBER 3, 1802

Earth has not anything to show more fair:
Dull would he be of soul who could pass by
A sight so touching in its majesty:
This City now doth, like a garment, wear
The beauty of the morning; silent, bare,
Ships, towers, domes, theatres, and temples lie
Open unto the fields, and to the sky;
All bright and glittering in the smokeless air.
Never did the sun more beautifully steep
In his first splendour, valley, rock,, or hill;
Ne'er saw I, never felt, a calm so deep!
The river glideth at his own sweet will:
Dear God! the very houses seem asleep;
And all that mighty heart is lying still!

William Wordsworth

I WANDERED LONELY AS A CLOUD

I wandered lonely as a cloud
That floats on high o'er vales and hills,
When all at once I saw a crowd,
A host, of golden daffodils;
Beside the lake, beneath the trees,
Fluttering and dancing in the breeze.

Continuous as the stars that shine
And twinkle on the milky way,
They stretched in never-ending line
Along the margin of a bay:
Ten thousand saw I at a glance,
Tossing their heads in sprightly dance.

The waves beside them danced; but they
Out-did the sparkling waves in glee:
A poet could not but be gay,
In such a jocund company:
I gazed - and gazed - but little thought
What wealth the show to me had brought:

For oft, when on my couch I lie
In vacant or in pensive mood,
They flash upon that inward eye
Which is the bliss of solitude;
And then my heart with pleasure fills,
And dances with the daffodils.

William Wordsworth

MY HEART LEAPS UP WHEN I BEHOLD

My heart leaps up when I behold
A rainbow in the sky:
So was it when my life began;
So is it now I am a man;
So be it when I shall grow old,
Or let me die!
The Child is father of the Man;
And I could wish my days to be
Bound each to each by natural piety.

William Wordsworth

ODE: INTIMATIONS OF IMMORTALITY FROM RECOLLECTIONS OF EARLY CHILDHOOD

X

Then sing, ye Birds, sing, sing a joyous song!
And let the young Lambs bound
As to the tabor's sound!
We in thought will join your throng,
Ye that pipe and ye that play,
Ye that through your hearts today
Feel the gladness of the May!
What though the radiance which was once so bright
Be now for ever taken from my sight,
Though nothing can bring back the hour
Of splendour in the grass, of glory in the flower;
We will grieve not, rather find
Strength in what remains behind;
In the primal sympathy
Which having been must ever be;
In the soothing thoughts that spring
Out of human suffering;
In the faith that looks through death,
In years that bring the philosophic mind.

XI

And O, ye Fountains, Meadows, Hills, and Groves,
Forebode not any severing of our loves!
Yet in my heart of hearts I feel your might;
I only have relinquished one delight
To live beneath your more habitual sway.

I love the Brooks which down their channels fret,
Even more than when I tripped lightly as they;
The innocent brightness of a new-born Day
Is lovely yet;
The Clouds that gather round the setting sun
Do take a sober colouring from an eye
That hath kept watch o'er man's mortality;
Another race hath been, and other palms are won.
Thanks to the human heart by which we live,
Thanks to its tenderness, its joys, and fears,
To me the meanest flower that blows can give
Thoughts that do often lie too deep for tears.

William Wordsworth

A CELTIC BLESSING

Deep peace of the running wave to you,
Deep peace of the flowing air to you,
Deep peace of the quiet earth to you,
Deep peace of the shining stars to you,
Deep peace of the Son of Peace to you.
May the road rise to meet you;
May the wind be always at your back;
May the sun shine warm upon your face;
May the rains fall softly upon your fields.
Until we meet again,
May God hold you in the hollow of His hand.

Anonymous

IF TEARS COULD BUILD A STAIRWAY

If tears could build a stairway
And memories were a lane
I would walk right up to heaven
And bring you back again

No farewell words were spoken
No time to say goodbye
You were gone before I knew it
And only God knows why

My heart still aches with sadness
And secret tears still flow
What it meant to lose you
No one will ever know

But now I know you want me
To mourn for you no more
To remember all the happy times
Life still has much in store

Since you'll never be forgotten
I pledge to you today
A hallowed place within my heart
Is where you'll always stay

Anonymous

NOT, HOW DID HE DIE, BUT HOW DID HE LIVE

Not, how did he die, but how did he live?
Not, what did he gain , but what did he give?
These are the units to measure the worth
Of a man as a man , regardless of birth.
Not what was his church, nor what was his creed?
But had he befriended those really in need?
Was he ever ready, with word of good cheer,
To bring back a smile, to banish a tear?
Not what did the sketch in the newspaper say,
But how many were sorry when he passed away?

Anonymous

THE UNQUIET GRAVE

The wind doth blow today, my love,
And a few small drops of rain;
I never had but one true-love;
In cold grave she was lain.

'I'll do as much for my true-love
As any young man may;
I'll sit and mourn all at her grave
For a twelvemonth and a day.'

The twelvemonth and a day being up,
The dead began to speak:
'O who sits weeping on my grave,
And will not let me sleep?'-

'Tis I, my love, sits on your grave,
And will not let you sleep;
For I crave one kiss of your clay-cold lips,
And that is all I seek.'-

'You crave one kiss of my clay-cold lips;
But my breath smells earthy strong;
If you have one kiss of my clay-cold lips,
Your time will not be long.

'Tis down in yonder garden green,
Love, where we used to walk,
The finest flower that ere was seen,
Is wither'd to a stalk.

'The stalk is wither'd dry, my love,
So will our hearts decay;
So make yourself content, my love,
Till God calls you away.'

Anonymous

TRADITIONAL GAELIC BLESSING

May the road rise up to meet you,
May the wind be always at your back.
May the sun shine warm upon your face;
May the rains fall soft upon your fields and until we meet again,
May God hold you in the hollow of his hand.

Anonymous

WESTERN WIND, WHEN WILL THOU BLOW

Western wind, when will thou blow,
The small rain down can rain?
Christ! if my love were in my arms,
And I in my bed again!

Anonymous

WHEN I AM DEAD, CRY FOR ME A LITTLE

When I am dead,
Cry for me a little,
Think of me sometimes
But not too much

Think of me now and again
As I was in life at some moment
That is pleasant to recall -
But not too long.

Leave me in peace
And I shall leave you in peace.
And whilst you live
Let your thoughts be with the living.

Indian Prayer

<u>ACKNOWLEDGEMENTS:</u>

To the best of my knowledge, the copyright has expired on all the long established poems herein.
M.A*.*

Made in the USA
Middletown, DE
14 March 2018